Cleansed by Christ

50 DEVOTIONS
FOR YOUR EMOTIONS

MISSY DUCHARME

TRILOGY

PROFESSIONAL PUBLISHING MEETS POWERFUL PROMOTION

A wholly owned subsidiary of **TBN**

Trilogy Christian Publishers
A Wholly Owned Subsidiary of Trinity Broadcasting Network
2442 Michelle Drive
Tustin, CA 92780

For information, address Trilogy Christian Publishing
Rights Department, 2442 Michelle Drive, Tustin, Ca 92780.

Trilogy Christian Publishing/ TBN and colophon are trademarks of
Trinity Broadcasting Network.

For information about special discounts for bulk purchases, please
contact Trilogy Christian Publishing.

Manufactured in the United States of America

10 9 8 7 6 5 4 3 2 1

Library of Congress Cataloging-in-Publication Data is available.

ISBN 979-8-89041-143-3
ISBN 979-8-89041-144-0 (ebook)

Dedication

First and foremost, I would like to thank God. Without Him I am nothing. I want to thank my daughter Juliet for being such a loving, smart, and supportive young lady. Even though my daughter Emma Rose is not here in the physical world, her love is with me every day and I am grateful that God blessed me with her as well. Thank you to my mother for always leading me closer to Christ. Thank you to all my incredibly supportive family and friends for all your encouragement along the way. I am truly grateful for each and every person that God has placed in my path. Each of you has helped me to learn and grow no matter what the circumstances may have entailed. I hope this book blesses each of you on your own journeys with Christ. Please always feel free to reach out and let me know how I can pray for you. You can contact me by subscribing to my email list at **bcharmedmusic.com**.

God bless!

Missy

I can do all things through Christ
who strengthens me.
Philippians 4:13

The love of Jesus Christ is enough despite your
circumstances. Anything is possible with Christ.

Table of Contents

Cleansed by Christ

50 Devotions
For your emotions

Missy Ducharme

Admiration

Finally, brothers and sisters, whatever is true,
whatever is noble, whatever is right, whatever is
pure, whatever is lovely, whatever is admirable,
if anything is excellent or praiseworthy
think about such things.

Philippians 4:8

It is important for us to remember to show our admiration
for God first above all else. This verse is also an important
reminder to have the same kind of respect for all the things
that God has created for us. He wants us to intentionally
focus our thoughts on these things.

Envy

A tranquil heart gives life to the flesh,
but envy makes the bones rot.

Proverbs 14:30

Having a tranquil heart can lead to greater fulfillment and happiness in your life because of the peace it instills within you. Envy can be very destructive; it ignites feelings of jealousy and malice, which can cause destructive behaviors. God calls us to live in peace with Him living in our hearts.

Triumph

But thanks be to God, who in Christ always
leads us to triumphal procession, and
through us speeds the fragrance of the
knowledge of Him everywhere.

2 Corinthians 2:14

God always wants to lead us to victory. The best way to get
there is to follow Him and let Him lead us there. Each time we
are triumphant in Him, His love shows through us and others
who love Him recognize it.

Patient

Be still before the Lord and wait patiently for
Him: do not fret when people succeed in
their ways, when they carry out
their wicked schemes.

Psalm 37:7

Not all timing is created equal. Sometimes we can see people advancing long before we do. They get married, buy a house, have children, and establish a successful career. But these things are not the measure of your worth, nor do they define who you are in Christ. Your time is coming. It's just not always in your timetable. Your blessing may also look very different than someone else's but that does not mean that you are not blessed. Even if you feel like someone doesn't deserve all that they have, be grateful for what God has in store for you. He has a plan for you. Trust His timing; it's always perfect.

Humble

Be completely humble and gentle, be patient
bearing with one another in love.

Ephesians 4:2

To be humble is not only to have a modest opinion of yourself,
but also to acknowledge others' value and contributions.
Everyone has their own strengths and weaknesses. God
wants us to genuinely try to understand each other. Humility
requires love, respect, kindness, and empathy. We can build a
stronger community and be stronger in Christ by remaining
humble.

Confident

Being confident of this He who began a good work in you will carry it on to completion until the day of Jesus Christ.

Philippians 1:6

Being confident in what God has planned for you can bring your life a sense of peace and purpose. It means trusting that God has a unique path for you and that everything that happens is for your good and His glory. Be confident in who He is and what He is capable of, and it will ultimately lead you to a fulfilled purpose with great joy.

Encourage

Therefore encourage one another and build
one another up, just as in fact you are doing.

I Thessalonians 5:11

Everyone is born with certain gifts, and I believe encouragement
is one of my gifts. I encourage you to try encouraging someone
today. Tell them they look pretty, be their cheerleader for the
new job they are beginning, let them know they are capable
of more than they think they are, tell them you are praying for
them. These are just a few small things you can do that could
make all the difference in the world to someone. It's how you
make a person feel that has the most lasting impact. God loves
when we are working in His favor.

Grief

For Godly grief produces a repentance that leads to salvation without regret, whereas worldly grief leads to death.

2 Corinthians 7:10

Whether your grief is rooted in sorrow or remorse for wrongdoings, it is a commitment to continue to hand it over to God. Those who call on Him will not have to carry the weight of the burden of grief. Grief can take over your body physically, emotionally, and spiritually if you allow it to. God is merciful to those who seek His grace.

Judgment

If anyone hears my words and does not keep them, I do not judge them for I did not come to judge the world but to save it.

John 12:47

Jesus does not judge us. So why do we judge others? It is important to remember His teachings on this and what the consequences are for not obeying. His primary mission was salvation, not judgment. Our faith, our actions, and our obedience to Him leads us to achieve eternal life.

Persevere

You need to persevere so that when you have
done the will of God you will receive
what He has promised.

Hebrew 10:36

To persevere, you must be open to growth and be willing to transform and learn from your mistakes. It requires faith, patience, and trust in God, even when adversity strikes. God's love and grace will provide us with the strength we need to face anything. When we walk on His path, according to His will, it will lead us to all of His promises.

Adoration

You shall love the Lord your God with
all your heart, with all your soul,
and with all your strength.

Deuteronomy 6:5

There is no greater expression of gratitude for God's love
for us than to live out our lives for Him. Acknowledging His
power, and wisdom, and grace through worship, reverence,
and love for others is a beautiful expression of our devotion to
Him. Love God for who He is, not just for what He has done
for us. Give Him all the glory He deserves.

Disappointment

Peace I leave with you; my peace I give you. I
do not give to you as the world gives.
Do not let your hearts be troubled
and do not be afraid.

John 14:27

There are so many different disappointments that we may encounter throughout our lives. Maybe we didn't get the job we wanted, we had a relationship fail, or we didn't get picked for a school sport. Whatever the disappointment may be, we must try to look at it through a new lens. Is it possible that whatever has not gone our way is nothing more than a blessing in disguise? God is always protecting us. He has something better in store for you.

Calmness

The Lord himself will fight for you.
Just stay calm.
Exodus 14:14

Calm is not always an easy way to be, especially in the midst of our troubles. Our first reaction may be to lash out in anger or worry tirelessly, but neither will work in our favor. When prompted with conflict or anxiety, try to take a moment to breathe and remember who your God is. He is taking care of you, so let your hearts and your minds be calm in Him.

Pride

When pride comes, then comes disgrace,
but with humility comes wisdom.

Proverbs 11:2

Pride can be a dangerous thing. It can also cause a lot of damage to people you care about if you are not careful. God wants us to be humble. The glory always goes to Him. One of us is never above the other. We are all His children, and should care for each other as such.

Appreciation

Give thanks in all circumstances, for this is
God's will for you in Christ Jesus.

1 Thessalonians 5:18

Even when you are in the midst of your troubles there is
always something to be thankful for. For example, my car
broke down, but it can be fixed, and I am grateful I have a
car to drive. Food is so expensive to buy, but I have a job and
I am thankful I can buy food. The list can go on and on. The
blessings are all around us. We just have to be grateful for our
blessings despite our burdens.

Confusion

God is not the author of confusion
but of peace.

1 Corinthians 14:33

First and foremost, when you are not at peace with something, it is not from God. This can be so tricky to decipher. We tend to overthink things at times, which can make it more difficult to discern whether something is right for us or not. Take it to God. Ask Him to show you His will. If your gut says no, believe it. That's the Holy Spirit within you prompting you to walk away or telling you that this situation is not for you. God is for you. He will lead you in the right direction. Trust Him.

Submissive

Submit yourselves therefore to God.
Resist the devil, and he will flee from you.
James 4:7

To be submissive to the will of God means acknowledging His sovereignty and trusting His plan rather than your own. We must align our lives and our actions with what He has taught us. Live according to His commandments. Fully submitting to God requires deep, abiding faith and a willingness to let go of our own agendas. Trust in Him. He is your biggest defense against the devil.

Amusement

And the streets of the city will be filled with
boys and girls playing in its streets.
Zechariah 8:5

God wants us to live joyful lives. When we allow ourselves to
play like children, we feel a sense of enchantment and wonder.
This allows us to see the world through a lens of hope and
beauty and helps us let go of some of the trials in our lives. It
is deeply fulfilling to embrace child-like love in our lives. God
provides us with an abundance of this kind of love.

Compassion

Therefore as God's chosen people, holy
and dearly loved, clothe yourselves with
compassion, kindness, humility,
gentleness, and patience.

Colossians 3:12

Jesus is the perfect example of what it means to be
compassionate. He lived His life devoted to His Father by fully
loving others with kindness and understanding despite their
background or circumstances. We should all try to live our
lives a little more like Christ. Be a light to the world and show
His love through our actions towards others. See others as
God sees them and respond with kindness and love.

Boredom

Whatever you do, work heartily,
as for the Lord, and not for men.
Colossians 3:23

Sometimes the daily aspects of our lives can seem so tedious and mundane. We must think of this as an opportunity to grow our relationship with Christ. Instead of letting boredom lead us to distractions, we can use this time to reflect, pray, and develop new ways to serve others and deepen our faith. When boredom creeps in, ask God to reveal any area of your life that might need a change. Working on His behalf has the greatest reward.

Self-Control

A man without self-control is like a city broken
into and left without walls.

Proverbs 25:28

When we rely on Christ's teachings and submit our thoughts,
actions, and behaviors to Him we are practicing self-control.
We must live our lives in a way that honors God and serves His
purpose. It is easier to overcome obstacles and resist sinful
behaviors when we are living to please Him. Jesus himself is
a perfect example of self-control. We should all try to emulate
His example so that we may develop the discipline we need to
live a life with meaningful purpose.

Anger

Whoever is slow to anger has great
understanding, but he who has a
hasty temper exalts folly.

Proverbs 14:29

It is ok to have the emotion of anger; it is not considered a sin. We are called to not let anger control us and not to let it lead to bitterness or hurtful behaviors. God encourages us to reconcile, forgive, and speak with love. We need to try to give others the same grace and compassion that He gives us. When you live your life filled with His Spirit, you are filled with peace.

Hunger

Jesus said to them, "I am the bread of life; whoever comes to me shall not hunger, and whoever believes in me shall not thirst."

John 6:35

To hunger for Christ means to long for a deep, abiding relationship with Him. It is a spiritual hunger that sustains and nourishes us in all aspects of our lives. A life with Christ means that we will experience what it is like to have true fulfillment and purpose. This transcends physical hunger and leads us to a life that honors God and serves others.

Courageous

Have I not commanded you? Be strong and courageous. Do not be frightened and do not be dismayed for the Lord your God is with you wherever you go.

Joshua 1:9

Sometimes we want to take matters into our own hands, and we allow fear to inhibit us. To be courageous requires us to step out in faith and trust in God and all His promises even when we face uncertainties. With God, we can overcome any obstacle and accomplish great things for His glory. Trust that the Lord is with you always. He has not forsaken you.

Satisfaction

For He satisfies the longing soul, and the
hungry soul He fills with good things.

Psalm 107:9

God satisfies our souls by providing us with everything we
need that transcends the material world. His unconditional
love, grace, wisdom, and peace offer us an abundance of
blessings we could never obtain anywhere else. We are blessed
beyond measure that He provides this type of fulfillment in our
lives. There is no greater satisfaction.

Anxiety

Do not be anxious about anything, but in every situation, by prayer and petition, with thanksgiving, present your request to God. (NIV)

Philippians 4:6

Anxiety is not an easy thing to overcome. Unfortunately, it can be a hindrance to our faith and allows a space for the devil to tell his lies. When we take our anxieties to God through prayer and thanksgiving, we shift our focus to Him rather than the problem. This gives us the peace and comfort we need to overcome our worries. Surrender it all to God and He will give you the strength, wisdom, and courage you need to live free from your anxieties.

Pure

Blessed are the pure in heart,
for they shall see God.
Matthew 5:8

It will be obvious to the world around you if you are living with a pure heart. You are choosing to live a life that is selfless, free from malice and deceit. A pure heart is not corrupted or affected by the world around them. Instead, they try to live a life filled with kindness, love, empathy, and service to others. God sees those who are genuinely of a pure heart, and He will surely reward them with His blessings. Those of pure heart see God in everything.

Cheerful

A glad heart makes a cheerful face, but by
sorrow of heart the spirit is crushed.

Proverbs 15:13

There is value in having a cheerful attitude. When we choose
to put things in a positive light rather than focusing on our
problems, we demonstrate our trust in God. When we are filled
with God's love, it reflects our inner soul that is aligned with
His goodness. Through this, we can be an encouragement to
others and live a joyful and fulfilling life.

Fear

Do not fear, for I am with you; do not be dismayed, for I am your God. I will strengthen you, I will help you; I will uphold you with my righteous right hand.

Isaiah. 41:10

Fear can take over if you allow it to. It can also inhibit you from doing the things that God has planned for you. It's a false sense of something going wrong. God repeatedly instructs us not to fear. We can trust that He is always with us and that He is bigger than any problem or challenge we may face. When we surrender our fears to Him, He will guide us and protect us against anything that may come our way. God is our peace and security, and He is holding our hand through it all.

Awe

Let all the earth fear the Lord; let all the
inhabitants of the world stand
in awe of Him.
Psalm 33:8

To stand in awe of God gives us a profound sense of reverence
and wonder. Recognizing His infinite power and wisdom over
all of creation is the most humbling experience we can have.
Trust that there are no limitations that can stop Him from
helping you. He is ultimately in control and your life will be
enriched because of it.

Nostalgia

They will still bear fruit in old age, they will
stay fresh and green[...] (NIV)
Psalm 92:14

It is not uncommon to look back on our youth and think that those were the best days that we are going to have. We should also remember to embrace the present and look forward to what God has in store for us. We can continue to make a positive impact regardless of our age or circumstances. Believe in God's plan for your life. As long as you are here, He will continue to fulfill His promises and bear fruit.

Sadness

Let us not become weary in doing good, for at
the proper time we will reap a harvest
if we do not give up. (NIV)

Galatians 6:9

One of the quickest and best ways to relieve our sadness is by doing good for others. It's ok to be sad sometimes, but it is important not to let it overtake us and overshadow the good we can do for others. If you are missing someone, do something in their honor; if you are feeling lonely, volunteer at a local shelter; if you are feeling unworthy, pay a compliment to someone else. All these things and more can shift our perspective off ourselves and onto making a meaningful difference in someone else's life. Faith, perseverance, and a willingness to serve God will surely please the Lord.

Guilt

If we confess our sins, He is faithful and just
to forgive us our sins, and cleanse
us from all unrighteousness.

1 John 1:9

We do not have to carry the burden of guilt alone. When we confess our sins to God, He promises to forgive us and cleanse us from all unrighteousness. It is difficult to fully embrace God's love and grace when we continue to carry the heavy weight of guilt. When we seek forgiveness, we can be free from that burden and experience the peace of God within us. No one is perfect and we all make mistakes, but through God's grace and mercy we can be restored.

Relief

To the choirmaster with stringed instruments. A Psalm of David. Answer me when I call, Oh God of my righteousness. You have given me relief when I was in distress. Be gracious to me and hear my prayer.

Psalm 4:1

We often seek relief because we are in distress or amid difficult circumstances. Please know that we can all turn to God and He will hear our prayers and answer our call with mercy. We are never alone, and God can provide relief in many forms. Whether it be through music, prayer, or simply placing our complete trust in Him, He will guide us and support us every step of the way.

Desire

Charm and grace are deceptive, and beauty is vain, but a woman who fears the Lord shall be praised.
Proverbs 31:30

Our desires should be based on what is lasting and meaningful rather than on superficial things such as beauty and charm. When we desire a deep, abiding relationship with the Lord, we gain so much more wisdom and purpose, which transcend all the other worldly pleasures. Wouldn't you rather be known and respected for your character and virtue than for anything superficial? To live according to God's will should be our only desire.

Joy

The joy of the Lord is your strength.
Nehemiah 8:10

Joy is not dependent on external factors such as success, wealth, or material things, but rather true joy comes from the relationship we have with God. When we focus on the joy of the Lord, we can experience a sense of purpose and fulfillment through all the challenges we experience. When we deepen our relationship with God, joy becomes a state of being. The joy of the Lord makes us stronger.

Wrath

Beloved never avenge yourselves, but leave it to the wrath of God, for it is written, " Vengeance is mine, I will repay says the Lord."

Romans 12:19

Wrath is a powerful emotion, and it can consume us if we allow it to. It is important for us to trust in God and His sovereignty. He will deal with the wrongdoings and those who have hurt us. It's not up to us to handle them. He will make the wrong things right. God wants us to respond in love and forgiveness, not anger. He is our vindicator.

Awkwardness

God knows everything about you, including the anxious thoughts you have when you need to be social with others. Your anxious thoughts do not turn Him off, nor do they evoke His irritation or ire against you.

Psalm 139:23

If you are introverted or on the shy side, you may struggle with awkwardness. Social situations may seem like a mountain to climb. In these times of discomfort, rest assured that God is with you. He knows every hair on your head, every flaw, and every perfectly imperfect thing about you, and still loves you unconditionally. God loves us as we are. So, when the awkwardness sets in, rely on Him and He will provide all the confidence and grace you need.

Love

Love is patient, love is kind. It does not envy,
it does not boast, it is not proud. It does not
dishonor others, it is not self-seeking, it is not
easily angered, it keeps no record of wrongs.
Love does not delight in evil but rejoices with
the truth. It always protects, always trusts,
always hopes, always perseveres. (NIV)

1 Corinthians 13:4-7

God is love. Our love should reflect God's love. Love is not just a feeling but a choice and an action. This type of love is selfless, compassionate, forgiving, and enduring. Choosing to love others in this way honors God and the love He has for us. Showing others we love them through consistent acts of kindness, service, and sacrifice can be much more meaningful than mere words could ever be. It shows that we are willing to put their needs before our own. God is the ultimate source of love. There is no greater love that we could emulate than His.

Hopeful

"For I know the plans I have for you," declares
the Lord, "plans to prosper you and not harm
you, plans to give you hope and a future."
(NIV)

Jeremiah 29:11

Hope gives us the strength we need to persevere through difficult times even when we feel like giving up. Hope gives us a sense of purpose, comfort, and encouragement even when we don't fully know what lies ahead. God is the source of our hope, and we can trust that He is working all things together for our good.

Contempt

Whoever oppresses the poor shows contempt
for their maker, but whoever is kind to the
needy honors God. (NIV)

Proverbs 14:31

The way we treat others reflects our relationship with God.
If you mistreat or show disrespect toward the poor, you are
not only showing contempt towards them, but you are also
showing contempt towards God. He is our Maker. Treating
others with kindness, compassion and respect honors Him.
We need to remind ourselves that we are all created equal in
God's eyes.

Deceitful

The heart is deceitful above all things and desperately sick; who can understand it?

Jeremiah 17:9

We are all capable of this in some respects. We can even deceive ourselves if we are not careful with whom we share our hearts. The heart can play tricks on you and before you know it, you are justifying wrongdoings or unethical actions. Deceit can break trust and ruin relationships. It is up to us to strive to be honest, completely transparent and mindful of our actions to develop the relationships God wants us to have. We can build stronger and more authentic love, filled with integrity, when we honor God with our honesty.

Romance

Above all keep loving one another earnestly,
since love covers a multitude of sins.

1 Peter 4:8

God doesn't want us to get lost in the physical sense of romance. He wants us to remember that romance is a way to express deep selfless love to one another. If we prioritize kindness, forgiveness, and compassion for one another, we create a space for growth and a genuine intimate relationship. Love truly conquers all.

Empathy

God has given each of you a gift from His great variety of spiritual gifts. Use them well to serve one another. (NLT)

1 Peter 4:10

Empathy is an awareness of someone else's feelings and emotions without judgment or disdain. When we empathize with someone, we give them a safe space to be vulnerable and the ability to fully express themselves without the expectation of changing themselves. It allows people to be authentic and to feel seen and heard. This is one of the greatest spiritual gifts God has given us to serve each other well.

Disgust

And the Lord saw with disgust the evil-doing
of His sons and daughters.
Deuteronomy 32:19

Typically, disgust is a strong aversion or revulsion towards
something or someone. In this verse, God is expressing His
disgust towards the disobedience and sinfulness of His sons
and daughters. Despite His disappointment, He always offers
forgiveness and grace to those who seek to repent. In a world
full of darkness, be the light that God intended you to be.

Craving

And since you delight in obedience, do not shape your lives by the cravings which used to dominate you in your time of ignorance.

1 Peter 1:14

A craving is a powerful desire for something, which can also be viewed as a temptation. God is asking you to learn from your past mistakes and not to repeat them. In your obedience to Him, you will not be overtaken by your temptations. You can serve Him and others well by choosing not to give in to those cravings. The temptations will subside in your obedience to the Lord.

Yearn

For God is my witness, how I yearn for you all
with the affection of Jesus Christ.

Philippians 1:8

Our lives would be better served with an intense longing to know and serve our Lord. To live like Jesus is to live in a manner worthy of the gospel. God wants us to grow spiritual relationships with one another and build a community of believers that yearn for Him rather than for the things of this world.

Excitement

Then the people rejoiced because they had given willingly, for with a whole heart they had offered freely to the Lord. David the king also rejoiced greatly.

I Chronicles 29:9

What are some of the things that we get excited about? Is it a new job, a new house, or a baby on the way? There is nothing wrong with expressing excitement about any of these things, and God delights in our joyfulness. When we are giving willingly with our whole hearts and offer our time, talents, and efforts to God and His Kingdom, we can experience the most fulfilling sense of excitement there is. There is tremendous joy in being a part of something bigger than ourselves.

Sympathy

Finally, all of you, have unity in mind,
sympathy, brotherly love, a tender heart,
and a humble mind.

I Peter 3:8

It is important for us to show compassion and concern towards others, especially when they are experiencing loss or difficulties. We reflect God's love when we help to ease the burdens of one another. God is always there for us in our time of need, so He wants us to use our experiences to help guide someone else through their pain. Sympathy unifies us in Christ and is a great expression of love with a humble heart.

Peaceful

The peace of God, which transcends all understanding, will guard your hearts and your minds in Christ Jesus.

Philippians 4:7

To be in a peaceful state of mind you must trust in God despite what your mind can understand. The peace of God is not based on external circumstances; it comes from our relationship with Him and our trust in His sovereignty and goodness. We can face any challenge with courage and hope that will guard our hearts and minds with the peace of God. This is truly a gift.

CPSIA information can be obtained
at www.ICGtesting.com
Printed in the USA
JSHW010151150623
43256JS00003B/21

9 798890 411433